My
Guardian Angel
Prayer Book

Guardian Angel Prayer

Angel of God,
my Guardian dear
to whom God's love
commits me here.
Ever this day
be at my side
to light and guard
to rule and guide.
Amen.

My
Guardian Angel
Prayer Book

Is a Gift to

_____

Given with Love from

_____

On the Occasion of

_____

on

_____

My Guardian Angel Prayer Book

Edited by
REV. VICTOR HOAGLAND, C.P.

Illustrated by
WILLIAM LUBEROFF

Regina Press
New York

Imprimatur:
C. Eykens, Vic. gen.
Antverpiae, 30 junii 1990

THE REGINA PRESS
10 Hub Drive
Melville, New York

Printed in Hong Kong.

My Dear Child:

Guardian Angels are a sign of God's love and care for you and every child in all the world.

This small, first book of prayers has been given to you by someone who also loves and cares for you very much.

As you grow and learn the meanings of these beautiful prayers, may God's love always hold you close to Jesus' heart.

Fr. Victor

IMPORTANT PRAYERS

The Sign of the Cross

In the name of the Father
and of the Son
and of the Holy Spirit. Amen.

The Lord's Prayer

Our Father, who art in heaven,
hallowed be Thy name;
Thy kingdom come;
Thy will be done on earth
as it is in heaven.
Give us this day
our daily bread;
and forgive us our trespasses
as we forgive those
who trespass against us
and lead us not into temptation,
but deliver us from evil. Amen.

The Hail Mary

Hail Mary, full of grace.
The Lord is with thee.
Blessed art thou amongst women,
and blessed is the fruit
of thy womb, Jesus.
Holy Mary, Mother of God,
pray for us sinners,
now and at the hour
of our death. Amen.

Glory Be

Glory be to the Father,
and to the Son,
and to the Holy Spirit,
as it was in the beginning,
is now, and ever shall be,
world without end. Amen.

The Apostles' Creed

I believe in God the Father Almighty, Creator of heaven and earth; and in Jesus Christ, His only Son, our Lord; who was conceived by the Holy Spirit, born of the Virgin Mary, suffered under Pontius Pilate, was crucified, died, and was buried; He descended into hell; the third day He rose again from the dead; He ascended into heaven, and is seated at the right hand of God the Father almighty; from thence He shall come to judge the living and the dead. I believe in the Holy Spirit; the holy Catholic Church; the Communion of Saints; the forgiveness of sins; the resurrection of the body; and life everlasting. Amen.

Act of Contrition

O my God,
I am heartily sorry
for having offended You,
and I detest all my sins,
because of Your just punishments,
and most of all
because they offend You, my God,
who are good
and deserving of all my love.
I firmly resolve,
with the help of Your grace.
to sin no more
and to avoid the near occasions
of sin. Amen.

Act of Faith

O my God, I believe that You are one God in three Divine Persons: Father, Son and Holy Spirit. I believe that Your Divine Son became Man and died for our sins, and that He will come again to judge the living and the dead. I believe these and all truths that the Catholic Church teaches, because You have revealed them, who can neither deceive nor be deceived. Amen.

Act of Hope

O my God, relying on Your almighty power and infinite mercy and promises, I hope to obtain pardon of my sins, the help of Your grace and life everlasting through the merits of Jesus Christ, my Lord and Redeemer. Amen.

Act of Love

O my God, I love You above all things with my whole heart and soul, because You are all good and worthy of all love. I love my neighbors as myself for the love of You. I forgive all who have injured me and ask pardon of all whom I have injured. Amen.

Here is a prayer to Mary, the Mother of Jesus. In it, we beg her to pray for us.

Memorare

Remember, O most loving Virgin Mary, That never was it known that anyone who asked for your protection, or looked for your aid, or begged for your prayers, was left without help. As I think of this, I fly to you, O Virgin of Virgins, my Mother. To you I go, before you I kneel, filled with sorrow for my sins. Do not turn away from me, O Mother of Jesus, but hear me and pray for me to your son. Amen.

PRAYER TO JESUS

Soul of Christ

Soul of Christ, sanctify me,
Body of Christ, save me.
Blood of Christ, inebriate me.
Water from the side of Christ, wash me.

Passion of Christ, strengthen me.
O good Jesus, hear me.
Within your wounds, hide me.

Separated from you, let me never be.
From the malignant enemy, defend me.

At the hour of death, call me.
To come to You, bid me,
that I may praise You
in the company of Your saints,
for all eternity. Amen.

Morning Prayer

In the morning we thank God for keeping us safe all night. We thank Him for the new day. We offer Him everything we shall do and say and think.

A Morning Offering

O Jesus, I offer You everything
I shall do and say and think today.
I offer You my happy times
and my sad times.
I offer them so that all You want
may come to pass.
I join my prayers to those of Mary,
Your Mother, who is my mother,
too. Amen.

At Playtime

God wants us to be happy. When playtime comes, He wants us to enjoy it. Playtime should be a happy time for us and our friends. And so we ask God to help us be fair during our games. We offer Him the fun we shall have while we play.

Before Meals

Bless us, O Lord,
and these Your gifts,
which we are about to receive
from Your goodness,
Through Christ, our Lord.
May the Lord relieve the wants
of others. Amen.

Night Prayers

Before we go to bed, we thank God for the day that is past. We ask Him to bless all the people we love. We tell God we are sorry for any wrong we have done. We may say the Act of Contrition. We also may ask God to give us a good night's sleep and say the following prayer:

A Prayer for Bedtime

Now I lay me down to sleep,
I pray the Lord my soul to keep.
If I should die before I wake,
I pray the Lord my soul to take.
Amen.

The Stations of The Cross

The story is told that after Jesus ascended to heaven, His mother Mary retraced the steps of her son's passion. From time to time she would walk from the governor's house to Calvary along the same path taken by Jesus.

It is a good way to show Jesus how thankful we are for all He has done for us.

In your church you will see fourteen pictures around the walls. On each picture there is a cross and a number. The pictures, or stations, show Jesus on His way to Calvary. They show His death and burial. We walk from on station to another. We stop at each one. We think of what is happening in the picture. We do not have to say any prayers.

1st STATION

Jesus Is Condemned to Death

Jesus is brought before Pilate to be judged. He is innocent but he is condemned and taken away to be put to death.

2nd STATION

Jesus Takes Up His Cross

The cross is very heavy. Jesus knows it will be painful but He accepts it willingly to save us from our sins.

3rd STATION

Jesus Falls for the First Time

The heavy cross drives the thorns still deeper into His brow. Jesus is weak from the loss of blood. He falls and the soldiers roughly drag Him up again.

4th STATION

Jesus Meets His Mother

When Mary sees Jesus, her heart is broken. He is covered with dirt and blood. Mary weeps because He is suffering terribly and there is no way she can help Him.

5th STATION

Simon of Cyrene Helps Jesus

Jesus is so weak He can no longer carry the cross. The soldiers fear that He will faint or die on the way. So they ask a man named Simon to help Him.

6th STATION

Veronica Wipes the Face of Jesus

A good lady runs to Jesus and wipes His face with her veil. How she pitied Him and how anxious she was to do something for Him!

7th STATION

Jesus Falls the Second Time

Again Jesus staggers under the weight of the cross and falls heavily to the ground. The cruel soldiers, with kicks and blows, force Him to His feet again.

8th STATION

Jesus Meets the Women of Jerusalem

Jesus meets some women who are grieving and crying loudly. He tells them not to weep for Him but for all the sinners who will not repent and be saved.

9th STATION

Jesus Falls the Third Time

Jesus is now near the place where He will be fastened to the cross. He thinks of all the pain He must still suffer. All His strength leaves Him and He falls to the earth.

10th STATION

Jesus Is Stripped of His Clothes

The long journey to Calvary is now finished. The soldiers roughly tear off His clothes. Jesus is humiliated and treated like a common criminal.

11th STATION

Jesus Is Nailed to the Cross

At last, Jesus is placed upon the cross. The soldiers then drive nails through His hands and feet. The cross is then raised and placed into the earth.

12th STATION

Jesus Dies on the Cross

How patiently Jesus suffers. For three long hours His body hangs on the cross. He speaks kindly to the good thief. He lovingly talks to Mary. At last He bows His head and dies.

13th STATION

The Body of Jesus
Is Taken Down from the Cross

After His death, friends take Jesus down from the cross. Gently they lower His body into the arms of His mother, Mary. With great love she again holds her beloved son.

14th STATION

The Body of Jesus
Is Laid in the Tomb

The body of Jesus is placed in a tomb. Soldiers seal the tomb and block the entrance with a great stone. The followers of Jesus return to their homes to wait for Jesus to rise from the dead on the third day, as He promised.

Prayer Before A Crucifix

Look down upon me, good and gentle Jesus, while before Your face I humbly kneel and with burning soul pray and beseech You to fix deep in my heart lively sentiments of faith, hope and charity, true contrition for my sins, a firm purpose of amendment.

While I contemplate, with great love and tender pity, Your five most precious wounds, pondering over them within me and calling to mind the words which David, Your prophet, said of You, my Jesus:

'They have pierced my hands and my feet, they have injured all my bones." Amen.

The Rosary

The Rosary is made up of sets, or groups, of beads on a chain. In each set there is one big bead and ten small beads. Each set is called a decade.

On the big beads, we say the Our Father. On the small beads, we say the Hail Mary. After the last Hail Mary in a decade, we say a Glory Be. Before each decade, we think of something that happened to Jesus and Mary.

The Joyful Mysteries

1. The Annunciation
2. The Visitation
3. The Birth of Jesus
4. The Presentation of Jesus in the Temple
5. The Finding of Jesus in the Temple

The Sorrowful Mysteries

1. The Agony in the Garden
2. The Scourging of Jesus
3. The Crowning of Jesus with Thorns
4. The Carrying of the Cross
5. The Death of Jesus on the Cross

The Glorious Mysteries

1. The Resurrection
2. The Ascension
3. The Coming of the Holy Spirit
4. The Assumption of Mary
5. The Coronation of Mary in Heaven

The Ten Commandments

1. I, the Lord, am your God. You shall not have other gods besides me.

2. You shall not take the name of the Lord, your God, in vain.

3. Remember to keep holy the sabbath day.

4. Honor your father and your mother.

5. You shall not kill.

6. You shall not commit adultery.

7. You shall not steal.

8. You shall not bear false witness against your neighbor,

9. You shall not covet your neighbor's wife.

10. You shall not covet anything that belongs to your neighbor.

The Beatitudes

1. Blessed are the poor in spirit, for the kingdom of heaven is theirs.

2. Blessed are those who are sad, for they shall be comforted.

3. Blessed are the mild and gentle, for they shall inherit the land.

4. Blessed are those who hunger and thirst for justice, for they shall be filled.

5. Blessed are the merciful, for they shall receive mercy.

6. Blessed are the pure in heart, for they shall see God.

7. Blessed are those who make peace, for they shall be called the peacemakers.

8. Blessed are those who suffer for My sake, for heaven will be theirs.

What the Church Asks of Us

1. That we go to Mass on Sundays and holy days of obligation.

2. That we fast and abstain on the days appointed.

3. That we confess our sins at least once a year.

4. That we receive Holy Communion during Easter time.

5. That we contribute to the support of the Church.

6. That we observe the laws of the Church on marriage.

The Sacraments

The seven sacraments are special ways established by Jesus to help us live God's life more fully. Each sacrament brings with it a special grace from God.

They are:

1. Baptism

2. Confirmation

3. Holy Eucharist

4. Reconciliation

5. Anointing of the Sick

6. Holy Orders

7. Matrimony

Virtues
God's Gifts to Us

Faith -we believe all that God tells us.

Hope -we trust that God will always help us

Love -we love God and all people.

Gifts of the Holy Spirit

Wisdom   Knowledge

Understanding   Piety

Counsel   Fear of the Lord

Fortitude

The Chief Corporal
Works of Mercy

To feed the hungry.

To give drink to the thirsty.

To clothe the naked.

To visit the imprisoned.

To shelter the homeless.

To visit the sick.

To bury the dead.

Jesus said: *"As long as you did it for one of these, the least of My brethren, you did it to Me."*

The Chief Spiritual Works of Mercy

To admonish the sinner.

To instruct the ignorant.

To counsel the doubtful.

To comfort the sorrowful.

To bear wrongs patiently.

To forgive all injuries.

To pray for the living and the dead.

Jesus said: *"Judge not, and you will not be judged; condemn not, and you will not be condemned; forgive, and you will be forgiven."*

The Divine Praises

Blessed be God.
Blessed be His Holy Name.
Blessed be Jesus Christ,
    true God and true Man.
Blessed be the name of Jesus.
Blessed be His most Sacred Heart.
Blessed be His most Precious Blood.
Blessed be Jesus in the most
    Holy Sacrament of the altar.
Blessed be the Holy Spirit, the paraclete.
Blessed be the great Mother of God,
    Mary most holy.
Blessed be her holy and Immaculate
    Conception.
Blessed be her glorious Assumption.
Blessed be Joseph her most chaste spouse.
Blessed be God in His angels
    and in His saints.

A CHILD'S ALBUM
OF SAINTS

In his letters, Saint Paul referred to early Christians as Saints. According to him, everyone who believed in Jesus was a Saint. So Paul would have called you a child saint.

Through the centuries, the church has called Saints only those holy people who were canonized after their death. These Saints lived holy lives and usually performed miracles.

Catholics pray to Saints for special help and assistance. Saints are like good friends. They already live in heaven, but they also know what it is like to live on earth.

Saints sometimes help us directly, as good friends do. Or they can pray to God for us. Or they can join their prayers with ours to God.

There are two important things to remember about Saints.

First, they are already with God.

Second, they are most willing and eager to help you.

God is good, and will hear their prayers for you.

Here are some of the Saints you will want to know.

Saint Anthony

Saint Anthony is most known for helping find things that get lost. All through life, you will lose things. Whether it's something big or very little, ask Saint Anthony. And if he helps you find what you lost, be sure to say aloud, "Thank you, Saint Anthony!"

Dear Saint Anthony,
pray for me to Little Jesus,
whom you held lovingly
in your arms.
Obtain for me the grace to love him
with all my heart.
Amen.

Saint Francis

*Saint Francis was known for his love of
nature. He was able to talk to birds, fish and
other animals.*

Dear Saint Francis,
teach me to know
all the lovely creatures
that live in our world.
When I am tempted to be harsh,
help me to be gentle and kind.
Amen.

Saint Bernadette

Saint Bernadette was a little French girl, to whom Mary, the mother of Jesus, appeared at Lourdes. Mary told Bernadette "I am the Immaculate Conception." In the waters at Lourdes, where the vision happened, many miraculous cures have occurred.

Dear Saint Bernadette,
remember when
you were a young person
like I am?
Please tell Mary
that I am your friend.
I will come to you
and ask for special favors
when I need them.
Fill my life with grace.
I want to see Mary, too.
Amen.

Saint Joan of Arc

Saint Joan was a very brave young French woman. She often heard voices coming from God. They told her to lead her people to freedom. Her love for God was strong and pure.

Dear Saint Joan,
help me to be strong and pure
in my love of God. Help me
to listen closely to the words of God
and the ways He will touch my life.
Help me to be brave
in following God's call.
Amen.

Saint Martin De Porres

Saint Martin lived his life in Peru caring for the slaves who were brought to Peru from Africa. He had a special love for the sick and performed many miracles in his lifetime. He is the Patron of Social Justice.

Dear Saint Martin,
please pray for all those who suffer
because of prejudice
and discrimination.
When I think I am more important
to God than somebody else,
remind of your love
for the African slaves.
Amen.

Saint Therese of the Child Jesus

Saint Therese, also called the Little Flower, spent her life hidden in prayer. She dedicated her life to saving souls. Without ever leaving her convent, she became a missionary all over the world by the power of her prayers.

Dear Saint Therese,
help me to pray
fervently to God.
I want to remember to pray
for so many different people
and sometimes I forget.
Be my friend and lead me to God
and together we shall pray to Jesus
and Mary.
Amen.

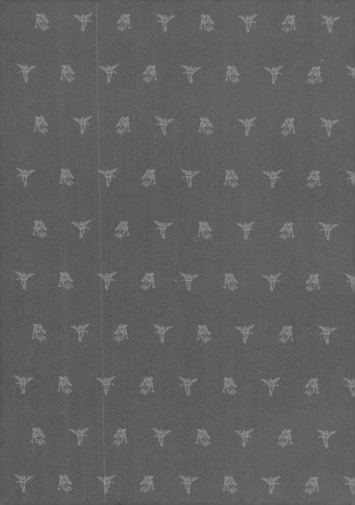